I'M AMERICAN:

IN THE LIGHT OF DAWN

L.C. RUSCH

DEFIANCE PRESS
& PUBLISHING

ISBN-13: 978-1-955937-43-6 (Paperback)
ISBN-13: 978-1-955937-42-9 (eBook)

Published by Defiance Press and Publishing, LLC

Bulk orders of this book may be obtained by contacting Defiance Press and Publishing, LLC at: www.defiancepress.com.

Public Relations Dept. – Defiance Press & Publishing, LLC
281-581-9300
pr@defiancepress.com

Defiance Press & Publishing, LLC
281-581-9300
info@defiancepress.com

Author's Note:

I'm American is written in tribute to my countrymen who lived through these events. The characters who appear in these stories are entirely fictional. Their experiences are based on historical accounts and channeled through research and imagination to create this final product. I hope you enjoy this flash of history and find yourself motivated to dig deeper into the history of our nation. For every American who came before me, thank you for the country I so joyously love.

L. C. Rusch

www.lcrusch.com

The *I'm American* Declaration

I believe in the strength of a country committed
to the principles of freedom

I believe in the pursuit of truth both past and present

I believe in the hope of the unknown future
and the endless possibilities

I believe in the power of hard work and determination

I believe in the love of community and family

I believe in the appreciation of teamwork and collaboration

I believe in the function of integrity and ethics

I believe in the respect of alternative opinions
and its necessity in a democracy

I believe in the fighting spirit and know that
what I do not stand for will fall

I believe in the reverence of sacrifice and memorial for those gone

I'm American

SEPTEMBER 22, 1711
THE COLONY OF NORTH CAROLINA

Gisella laughed and skipped away, ignoring her guilty heart. Mama could wait a few more minutes for the beautyberries. She hadn't seen her friends in days and she wanted to play while she still had the chance. All too soon, she might grow up and be stuffy and boring like her older brother, Malachi.

With determination she turned her face toward the road, letting the cool breath of an early autumn morning wake her. She followed John's quick pace down the road. Last night, he had stopped by to relay the message that all the neighboring kids were congregating in the southern meadow at dawn. Why she was not sure. But she was more than willing to accept a break in the usual days of drudgery, even if it meant slipping out of her house before sunrise.

John had been impatiently waiting for her at the crossroads, ready to be on his way. Though barely two years older than her ten years, John acted as if he were a full-grown adult, nodding his head sagely to the group of Tuscarora they passed in the last rays of moonlight.

It had taken nearly the full year since their settlement had begun for Gisella to become accustomed to the warriors presence. They had always been kind, easy to trade with, and nonaggressive. But they were different—different than her family and everyone else she spent time with—and their presence had always discomfited her.

"Hurry up, Gisella," said John with a huff. "They're going to pick teams without us."

Laughing, Gisella lengthened her stride, but it was still no match for John's growing legs. Instead, she picked up her petticoats and jogged at his side.

At the faster pace, it took only a few minutes for them to reach the open clearing. Gisella's eyes ran through the small group clustered there, halting when she saw Charlotte. Her friend broke away from the crowd, embracing her.

"It's about time you showed up. Matthew wanted to start without you."

Gisella glared at the offending boy, but he simply shrugged, unconcerned with the accusation. Gisella tried not to let his unaffected smugness annoy her; unfortunately, she had never been skilled at brushing off his attitude.

"But since we're on my land, I refused to allow it," Charlotte continued, grinning.

Gisella was relieved that her friend had seen fit to wait for her. With everyone's homes scattered about, it was an infrequent occurrence to congregate outside of a church function. "Then what are we waiting for?" she asked, smiling with anticipation.

Without hesitation, everyone began to break into teams and spread across the clearing. The laughter grew as the darkness eased. Gisella could practically feel her heart glowing in her chest, being at home with just her family could be so boring. But here she could talk to so many different people, she could never get bored—even if she had to sidestep Matthew a time or two.

The sun hadn't crested the treetops when the first scream tore through the air. It was high-pitched and stopped every kid in their tracks. Almost as one, they turned toward the noise—toward town. The scream echoed through the trees, seeming to come from different directions until Gisella realized there were multiple screams.

Her blood froze in her veins as the noises continued and multiplied. *Mama, Papa...* She tried to swallow, but her mouth felt as dry as a road in August, dusty and cracked.

For how long they stood there she had no idea, until movement caught the corner of her eye.

Matthew, the oldest present, was herding everyone toward the treeline. The serious expression he wore was foreign to her; gone was the irritating boy she had grown accustomed to.

"What is going on?" Gisella's whispered plea was barely audible amidst the screams that rang through the morning stillness. But the question pulled him up short as he approached her. Matthew's usually mischievous eyes were uncertain and scared.

"I don't know, but we need to get out of the open." He turned her shoulders toward the edge of the clearing and nudged her until she followed the others. She could count twelve making up their timid group.

He fell into step beside her, and she couldn't resist asking. "Should we head for town? Or to one of the farms?"

"I don't think it will be any use." His eyes were heavily shadowed.

Swallowing, she shoved down the grief and raw fear clawing at her throat. What about everyone she knew? Malachi? Her baby sister? Her fear stuttered as she caught up with Charlotte, whose face was pale as last winter's snow. Gisella put an arm around her friend as the shade of the trees caressed them.

Matthew led them farther into the shadowy forest until the clearing was no longer visible and trees surrounded them on every side. If only there were silence to accompany it.

Their entire group jumped as one when a similar cry broke out nearby—in the direction of Charlotte's home.

Charlotte looked toward home, her face paler than ever, then turned to Gisella with a white-knuckled grip on her skirt. Charlotte's mouth was moving, but no noise came out. Then, without warning, she took off, sprinting through the trees.

"Charlotte!" Gisella yelled, only to be shushed by Matthew. For once not caring what he thought, she took off running after her friend. She had no idea what was going on, but she knew her friend bursting into the middle of it wouldn't end well.

Her lungs burned as she raced through the trees, dodging branches. Charlotte wasn't a fast runner, and Gisella caught up with her just as the house became visible through the trees.

To her horror, three figures walked away from the tiny home, the blades hanging from their waists gleamed red in the light of dawn. A sob caught in Gisella's throat as she grabbed her friend and wrapped her in an embrace, less for comfort and more to stifle the sobs already bursting from her. "Shhh," she murmured. Gisella watched the figures circle the house, looking for anyone they might have missed. Her stomach flipped, knowing what lay inside.

"Mama, Papa, Mama, Papa…"

Charlotte's sorrowful mantra tore at Gisella's heart, and tears welled up in her eyes. She gripped her friend tighter, pulling her almost painfully close. She swallowed a scream as a hand landed on her shoulder.

Matthew's face was white with terror as he took in the figures investigating the farm. "We have to move." His breath was hot on her ear as he barely made any noise.

She nodded in acknowledgment before glancing pointedly at Charlotte. Her friend shook like the last leaf in a November wind.

Silently, Gisella stepped back, urging Charlotte to move with her, but her friend's legs only dragged in the underbrush. Muttering too softly to discern, Matthew stepped closer, pushing Gisella against a nearby tree.

Total silence met her ears as they huddled behind a thick oak. Even Charlotte had gone silent, her eyes becoming listless as she gazed at the bark digging into Gisella's back. Matthew's eyes, looking older than his thirteen years, tracked the figures in the distance.

Fear lit his face, and he pushed himself tighter against the tree, pressing Charlotte's dead weight deeper into Gisella's embrace. The latter's breath caught in her throat as Matthew's eyes tracked something moving to the side closer and closer to the edge of their barrier.

Gisella's breath hitched, and Matthew immediately raised a hand to her lips gently shushing her, his gaze conveying the severity of the need to maintain silence. Tears slid down her face as she nodded, her hand gripping one of his suspenders. She knew he wouldn't abandon them—otherwise, he never would have followed them—but gripping him a little closer helped to ease a tiny portion of the fear raking down her spine.

Their huddle of limbs jumped as a loud cry pierced the morning. It wasn't a sound of pain or fear but one of triumph. Though she had never heard it before today, Gisella knew what it was. A Tuscarora war cry.

Matthew wrapped his arms around both girls as the three figures she had seen leaving the cabin took up the call. The sound bounced off the trees, echoing all around her. The call was a break in the silence, and suddenly the air around them was filled with voices, none of which she could understand, though the cadence was familiar. She had heard it in town when the traders haggled with the Tuscarora.

As the voices faded away, headed in the direction of town, her heart chilled. She had heard that language just this morning. The group she and John had passed on the road.

Fear froze her tongue as she looked up at Matthew. His gaze was still fixed on where the figures must have disappeared.

Her tongue finally caught up with her brain. "Matthew," she whispered desperately.

His entire focus was on her in a blink. "What is it?" His words were quick and quiet.

"I just remembered…" Her voice wobbled, but they both ignored it. "John and I passed a group of Tuscarora on the way here."

Matthew's eyebrows slammed down. "Did they see you?"

"Yes, John greeted them." Her heartbeat picked up at the raw fear filling Matthew's eyes.

"We have to move. If they know we're out here…" He didn't finish, and Gisella didn't need him to. He pushed away from the haven of their hiding place, pulling Gisella and Charlotte with him.

Gisella stumbled a few steps before righting herself and her friend. "Come now, Charlotte. We have to go." Her friend shook her head fiercely, eyes searching for her home through the trees.

Tears drifted down Charlotte's face but she paid them no mind as her eyes darted around the surrounding area, her breathing becoming more and more erratic.

"They're all gone," Charlotte whispered, refusing to look at either of her companions.

"And if we don't move, we will be, too," Gisella pleaded, pulling her friend a few steps.

"So?"

"So, we're going to move." Spine stiffening in resolve, she met Matthew's urgent gaze a couple of paces away. With determined steps, she moved toward the crushed grass path they had made on their hasty arrival. With a firm arm around Charlotte's shoulders, she made her friend match her step for step.

They walked away. Away from Charlotte's home—from the family she would never see again and from the life they had known. Gisella tried not to imagine her own home, how a similar sight would greet her should she give into temptation and dash back now.

Screams and war cries pierced the air as they moved, Matthew prodding them faster until they nearly swept past where John and the others were huddled in the thorny underbrush.

There was no argument as Matthew roused the group, pulling them up from where they hid. They all knew what had happened to the settlement; they knew that braving the town would only result in more loss. There would be nothing left to salvage—no one to save.

Gisella stumbled across a fallen branch, as her eyes were too watery to see it in her path. But still, she moved; she held on to Charlotte and followed Matthew's lead. It wouldn't be an easy journey, but perhaps they would survive. And for a morning like today, she tried to be more grateful for that.

———

The sound of their feet in the underbrush wasn't enough to drown out the screams. Gisella pretended she could hear nothing as they moved past the meadow, where their games had begun. It seemed so long ago when they had been laughing and chasing each other.

A Tuscarora war cry rang out nearby but in the opposite direction of Charlotte's farm. Immediately, Matthew halted his progress, and they all came to a stop. They were surrounded.

Turning sharply, Matthew ushered them to a large clump of arrowwood bushes. They hid beneath its leafy canopy. He quietly called John and her aside. Neither Charlotte nor James answered when he motioned for them to join, their expressions vacant as they stared at the ground. "We're going to have to move very carefully if we're to survive." Matthew's eyes held a focused desperation that sank deep into Gisella's heart.

The focus was survival, and Gisella nodded sharply, latching on to the single goal. If she could make it her only concern, she could ignore the pain tearing through her chest.

"Being out in the open is dangerous," John whispered, and his eyes darted around as if expecting the trees to morph into attackers.

"Exactly." Matthew pointed to John in confirmation, and they all pretended they didn't notice how his hand shook. "So, we find cover, and we move slowly and carefully. We don't leave one area of cover until we have another in sight and even then, we go one by one."

"What about them?" Gisella tipped her head toward their small band of children. Some were watching their conversation indifferently; others were staring at nothing, not even a trace of fear in their expression. But they all shared the mark of tears, their eyes puffy and red. "They don't seem to fully comprehend the situation." Her lips pinched in a grimace.

"We tell them straight up bluntly what's going to happen," Matthew hesitated as his eyes scanned the group. "And if they still can't do it on their own, we help them. No one gets left behind." A note of finality ran through his softly-spoken words. Both Gisella and John nodded their agreement.

It took a few minutes to get everything sorted and for them to determine their next destination. Matthew murmured a few more instructions to John before they both slipped out. John immediately turned, his eyes surveying the forest to the north and east while Matthew moved cautiously south toward a clump of sycamore trees, his eyes facing south and west. Together, the two boys were able to see in every direction.

Matthew reached the grove of sycamore trees. They were packed tightly together and made for a good hiding spot. Once beside the trees, he gave the signal to Gisella.

In turn, she called up Silas. The lanky young boy had tearstains on his cheeks, and his eyes were dulled with pain. But when Gisella grabbed his hand and pointed to Matthew's location, he nodded, eyes intent and focused. Without a word, the young boy darted from the relative safety of their bushes and into the open. John and Matthew remained at their posts, eyes constantly scanning.

Gisella held her breath as Silas's light steps moved across the dry September dirt. When he was three steps from the sycamore trees, Matthew signaled again. This time, Gisella sent Martin, a boy her age whose baby round face was stricken with terror. He stumbled twice en route but arrived safely all the same.

The routine continued as they sent Winnie with James. The older boy's eyes were still listless, but Winnie's tiny hand gripping his own was enough to anchor his focus temporarily.

Elias was followed by George and another boy, only two years younger, named George. When it came to Charlotte's turn, Gisella did the same as she had done with everyone else. She held her hand and explained clearly what needed to be done. Charlotte nodded and stepped out of the shrubbery. Her first step was hesitant, her next stronger, as she moved through the trees. It was when she was halfway there that her feet stopped moving; her shoulders slumped and shook with sobs as she covered her face. For a moment, all was silent as Gisella hesitated. They were supposed to go one at a time, but she had a feeling Charlotte wouldn't be moving any farther on her own.

"Bring Rebecca with you," she murmured to John as she slipped from the arrowwood branches. Taking her steps gently, she made her way quickly to Charlotte. She didn't pause before her friend, simply wrapping her arm around her shoulders and moving forward. It gave Charlotte no time to protest; they couldn't afford to tarry any longer. With her friend having grown taller than

Gisella, the position was awkward but necessary.

Her stomach loosened slightly when they stepped into the shade of the sycamore grove. She barely had time to turn around before John and Rebecca arrived. With the group together once more, Matthew's eyes darted around the sullen faces. "We'll keep the same order from now; it'll be easiest to keep track of everyone that way." He glanced toward Charlotte for a moment before finding Gisella's gaze. She nodded in agreement. The last thing they needed was more confusion and someone getting left behind or wandering away.

"Good work everyone." Matthew attempted a smile but it did nothing beyond twist his lips into a grimace. "The next destination is those sycamores right there," he pointed a little farther away. Gisella was glad to see most of their group's heads turn in that direction, understanding their new goal.

Matthew led the way, each person following behind in the same order. Only the older of the Georges and Elias needed her prodding; everyone else was either fully focused on the task set for them or had been paired with someone else. James and Winnie stuck closely together as did Rebecca and John. Next to Gisella, Charlotte's entire body trembled as her eyes darted around as if the leaves hiding them had turned into knives.

The two girls made the trip together again, Gisella's grip tightening on Charlotte whenever she began to slow. Matthew pointed out their next shelter as a clump of sycamores, their bases overgrown with dogwood bushes. It would provide excellent shelter.

The pattern remained the same; it was only when Gisella and

Charlotte had taken two steps that they heard the voices. John's hand grabbed her free arm, pulling her back between the bases of three sycamore trees.

Her heart pounded in her throat as Matthew ducked into the branches of the bushes at the other end of their route. Their hiding place was a tight fit with John, Charlotte, Rebecca, and her sharing a space smaller than a chicken coop, but she didn't dare move.

A moment of silence ticked past, and Gisella prayed that the gentle wind had been the cause of concern. Perhaps a dead leaf had scraped against bark and created the noise.

But the next second, her prayer went unanswered. Unintelligible words reached their ears, growing louder with every heartbeat. Behind her, Rebecca's breath shuddered before she ducked her head between Gisella's shoulders. She could feel the little girl trembling, and her own breath wavered.

A loud shout made her heart stutter. She flinched sharply; it was so near. She refused to allow herself a glance at the encroaching Tuscarora, but it sounded as if they stood between her and Matthew. Their tiny group was separated by the very people who had forced them into flight this morning.

There was more discussion as their footsteps slowed to a halt. Gisella had never learned their language. The knowledge that they could be discussing her and her friends and she would have no idea sent a wracking shiver down her spine. They could be detailing how they would ambush the separated groups, and yet they would still have no warning when it happened.

Her trembling increased and her ears picked up on one familiar word: *firewater*. Rum, or "firewater" as it had been branded, was the Tuscarora's favorite item to trade for. If they were under its effects, she could only pray they would be less observant and might pass by without noticing them.

Her palms were slick with sweat as her leg began to cramp in its awkward position, but she refused to move. There was too much debris on the ground to risk even shifting.

Beyond the children's cover, the Tuscarora continued their discussion. It grew more intense, the words becoming harsher and more clipped. Finally, a loud exclamation sounded and silence followed it. Gisella's heart beat heavily as she waited, not knowing the reason for the harsh exchange.

When her lungs began to burn, she realized she had been holding her breath. She allowed only the shakiest intake as no one moved or spoke.

The crunch of leaves crinkled, and John's hand on her arm tightened fractionally. Two more sets followed the first, still not speaking. She prayed desperately for those hidden with Matthew as the steps moved in that direction. But they never paused.

The steps continued, moving farther away, and her breath came easier with each heartbeat. She had no idea which direction they were headed, her sense of direction had always been laughable, but she didn't care. They were moving away, and that was all that mattered. They hadn't seen either of the groups, and she could release her most grateful prayer.

Rebecca's head rose from her back as the footsteps fell out of hearing range and silence returned to the forest. When nothing had moved for several more minutes, Gisella turned to John. While only a few years older than herself and still younger than Matthew, his eyes looked far older as he met her gaze. Pressing a finger to his lips, he moved carefully forward.

Gisella held her breath as he stuck his head farther and farther out from their shelter. But when no resounding shouts came, her shoulders relaxed slightly. They truly were gone.

Without another word, John stepped out to his original position. Turning around, Gisella gathered Charlotte before she saw Rebecca still cowering against a tree trunk. Without thinking, she leaned over and pressed a kiss to her hair. It was a gesture Mama had done to her more times than she could count and it had always eased her worries. What she wouldn't give for Mama to give her one last kiss.

Holding back tears, she shook the thought from her mind. She couldn't focus on what she had lost today; she needed to focus on what could be salvaged. With that in mind, she stepped carefully from the trees, her eyes scanning every direction before moving forward.

In a minute, she was hidden in the dogwood bushes while John and Rebecca slipped in. For a moment, the entire group simply looked at each other. For most of them, grief raged raw in their gaze, but there was a flicker. A flicker of gratitude. A flicker of hope. If only they could ensure the hope wasn't in vain.

Without another word, Matthew moved on to the next spot, and they began their journey once more.

It felt like they had been walking for days, but the sun told Gisella it had only been one. The minutes passed at an achingly slow pace as she learned a new language. It was a language of looks and hand signals. She knew each moment that passed filled with silence equated to another moment of survival, but all she wanted to do was scream—something to change the eerie stillness blanketing their small band.

With soft steps, she led Charlotte by the hand to the next hiding place, keeping her eyes focused on Matthew. He, in turn, kept his eyes focused on the north and west while John watched the south and east. Together, they covered the entire area, ensuring their movements went unnoticed.

An aura of empty calm settled upon her as she walked, her thoughts running in circles. If she had only stayed home like Mama had told her to. If only she had been a good daughter like she was supposed to be, then maybe things would have been different. Maybe she could have made a difference. Or at the very least she would have died with them.

She shook her head, forcibly clearing the morose thoughts and focusing instead on the present. It was all that had gotten her to that point. Gisella knew she needed to keep her wits about her, as the attention of the group was waning. After hours of the same movements, the repetitive routine of hopping from one place of shelter to the next was losing its interest.

John entered the leafy bushes behind her, having to push Rebecca's head under a protruding branch when she nearly walked directly into it.

With everyone gathered together, there was a heavy pause— one with a weight behind it she hadn't felt since their near run-in with the Tuscarora. Matthew grimaced as he looked at Winnie leaning against James' shoulder and Silas resting heavily against Martin. "I'm not sure we can keep going." His voice betrayed his worry as he gazed through the leaves to the sky above. The sun had begun its descent but not enough that darkness would be threatening soon.

"No, we need to put more distance between us and home." John croaked the last word as if something were lodged in his throat.

"I agree. But if we keep moving like this, we're bound to be found." Matthew gestured to the group. "Our movements are growing clumsy; stealth is no longer an option."

Gisella shivered, understanding the predicament through their eyes. Either they continued on as before and risked any others in the forest hearing them. Or they stayed put for the night, not having put enough distance between them and their destroyed homes. Her heart increased its pounding. Not only were they still in danger, but any decision they made moving forward would put them in more danger.

"What if we carried them?" John's question brought her up short. She glanced at Matthew, interested in his response. There was a pause.

"It could work." Their leader's eyes scanned the group, assessing. "James…" The boy in question responded this time, a positive sign Gisella guessed. "You will need to carry Winnie from now on." Matthew's tone brooked no alternative, but James nodded nonetheless.

"John, you will keep with Rebecca, and Martin you will take George." He motioned to the correct boy of that name, whose eyes were only half open, staring at the ground he sat on. A long pause filled the air as Matthew focused on Silas, his eyes uncertain as he glanced toward Charlotte and her.

She had noticed his lack of assignment for Charlotte and she was grateful he had seen the same listlessness in her Gisella did.

She doubted Charlotte was capable of seeing to herself at the moment; the last thing she needed was someone else to be responsible for.

"Silas will go with me." The uncertainty in Matthew's voice gave her the courage to speak up.

"No, Silas can come with me." She straightened her shoulders determinedly.

It hadn't been lost on her that Matthew was always the one to lead the way. If there were any danger he would be the one to encounter it first, even if it were as simple as an animal trap. He put himself in that position to ensure their safety ahead of his own.

She was grateful for what he had chosen to do—the responsibility he had taken—but she wouldn't add another burden to his load.

"Are you sure?" Matthew glanced toward Charlotte meaningfully. Her friend gazed down at her hands, and Gisella wondered if she even heard them talking. All of her other attempts to whisper and direct her friend hadn't come to any fruition.

"Yes, I can carry him," she asserted with more confidence than she felt.

Without another word, Matthew ducked out from the branches and moved to the next stand of trees. The newly formed pairings followed in order. John's idea worked flawlessly as fewer feet crunched on twigs, and it took half the time for the ground to be covered.

When it came to her turn, Gisella grabbed Charlotte's hand and tucked it into her apron at the back of her waist. She squeezed Charlotte's hand into a fist around the fabric and caught her friend's roaming gaze. There was no spark or recognition there, but she pushed forward regardless. "Hold on tight," she said, punctuating each murmured word with a squeeze. After several repetitions, she let go. To her relief, Charlotte's hand stayed where it was.

Without another word, Gisella held out her arms to Silas. The boy, while lanky, was thankfully light as she lifted him into her arms. His long legs hung down brushing against her knees as she walked forward. Charlotte followed in her wake, not making a noise and not letting go of her apron.

They were inside the newest grove of trees in a moment. She debated whether or not to lower Silas to the ground while she was standing. But the heavy weight of him against her was enough to keep her still. The young boy needed rest. It had been a long day for them all.

Their progress sped up through the afternoon as the smaller legs were allowed to rest while being carried in arms or across backs. It wasn't long before most of them were sleeping or, at the very least, dazed and silent.

The sun sank lower, nearing the horizon, and Gisella's heartbeat sputtered as Matthew ducked out of their most recent shelter only to immediately motion for silence. Barely breathing, he slowly backed up two steps to hide in the shadow of the trees. He didn't join them; the disruption of the leaves and swaying branches would garner too much notice Gisella guessed.

Three times that day, the same instance had occurred. Each time, they had burrowed down in their current hiding place as frantic footsteps approached, grateful they were already hidden from sight. Twice, the steps had moved beyond their hearing; once, the

Tuscarora had been too close. Gisella's empty stomach turned over as she forced away the memory. Matthew had veered their next hideaway a far distance from the body, but it couldn't erase the sound of the body thumping lifelessly to the ground .

Her chest eased when Matthew gently shook his head and crept forward again. Like a trail of ducks doggedly following their mother, everyone followed in turn. Her heart ached at the wet cheeks greeting her every time someone turned their face to the light of the sun. She had always found joy and laughter in the presence of these kids, and now they would be tied together with grief.

As darkness stretched over the forest, her steps became more labored and she tripped over multiple roots, barely keeping her grip on Silas. Finally, Matthew didn't dart out the moment John and Rebecca joined them. As one, she felt the group sigh with relief.

"We stay here for the night." His voice felt loud after hours of silence in the group. "No one goes out of sight. We stay together at all times." His somber expression was met with nods and blank stares but not a hint of an argument.

Gisella took a moment to gauge their resting place. Now that she looked closely, she understood Matthew's appeal in resting here. They were amidst several clumps of overgrown arrowwood bushes, and their broad width would keep them well hidden through the night.

Murmurs sounded as the youngest of their motley crew were awoken by their transition to the ground. Gently, she lowered Silas to the earth. The young boy didn't wake at her movement, instead curling into the sun-warmed grass.

"Gisella…" Matthew's gentle voice, such a rarity before today, pulled her attention from Silas. "Will you help with collecting the berries?" He nodded his head toward a nearby small congregation of bushes. In the last whispers of sunlight, she could make out clumps of berries.

Her heart rose in relief. Tomorrow wouldn't be an easier day; they would need something to keep up their strength.

"Of course." She tripped clumsily over the words, her voice thick with disuse.

The sound of whimpering followed in their wake as they moved toward the bushes, Matthew's eyes as watchful as ever. She didn't need to turn around to know John was watching as well, keeping them safe. Her tired eyes found interest in her feet as they walked.

"What do we do now?" Gisella's voice held little volume.

"We continue on to the next settlement," Matthew replied.

Her feet throbbed at the answer; tomorrow would be a long day, indeed. Her tongue stumbled over her next question, wanting an answer but not wanting to recognize the reality. "Do you think anyone will be there?" Her voice trembled, and she focused on untying her apron as they neared the bushes.

"I don't know," Matthew commented. His hands reached out to halt hers as they twisted her apron tightly. "But I don't know what else to do." It was a sad admission, but Gisella was glad he didn't attempt to hide it.

Nodding, she turned her focus to the task at hand. The final rays of sunlight turned the berries magenta. Her breath stuttered at the sight. Beautyberries.

She brought a hand to her lips as she dissolved into tears.

She felt a gentle arm across her shoulders as she knelt before the bushes, almost as if in prayer.

She should have been there. She should have been picking berries or perhaps just awakening from sleep when the first cries sounded. When the weapons were unsheathed, she should have been there with them. With Mama and Papa, with Malachi and her baby sister. But now they were gone. She knew that as surely as she knew today would never be far from her mind.

"Breathe, Gisella," Matthew murmured, kneeling beside her. She tried to follow his advice, but her chest was too constricted to take a full breath.

"I was supposed to be picking them…" She let a finger graze the nearest berry. Its overripe plumpness dragged the branch low to the ground. "Mama needed them, but I didn't want to gather them." She hiccupped abruptly, ending her tearful confession.

"We were all supposed to be somewhere else."

The words settled in her stomach, easing the tightness. It didn't make it better, but perhaps it made it a little less terrible.

She nodded her head, and together they began to collect the beautyberries. If they saw each other's silent tears hitting the dirt, neither commented.

━━━━━━━━━━

The clear night was too peaceful for Gisella to find rest. The few stars that peeked through the bushes' sheltering leaves shone too brightly. Her heart ached nearly as much as her hip did on the unforgiving root she had laid down upon. No matter how she adjusted, the offending root refused to grant her comfort.

The sound of heavy breathing had filled the air for a long time before a sob broke the quiet. Sitting up, she glanced to her left to find Matthew already at the child's side. His hushed voice carried on a gentle breeze.

"I know it hurts," he murmured consolingly.

"I want Mama," the distraught child cried, her voice carrying much farther than Matthew's had. Gisella saw his shoulders tense, and he glanced around at the still sleeping group. She doubted waking everyone else was the main concern he had.

"Rebecca, I know it's hard, but we must stay quiet." Matthew's hand reached out hesitantly to brush her brow. The gentle touch was met with an increased volume of tears.

Before Matthew could respond, Gisella rose and picked her way across sleeping forms to their side. Her heart felt heavier than her feet, as she saw Rebecca's miserable expression. She didn't know what to say; there was no way to take away the pain. Instead, she did what her mother had always done.

Offering her arms to Rebecca, she was surprised at the ferocity with which the young child flung herself upon her. Her sobs were muffled against Gisella's neck. Without a thought, she imitated the motion she had seen Mama do with her baby sister nearly every night.

Stepping past Matthew, she paced across an open bit of grass before turning back and repeating the motion over and over. Tears slipped from her eyes as she walked, knowing Mama would never be there to guide her again.

After the first two tracks back and forth, Rebecca quieted to a mere sniffle. The wet spot on Gisella's shoulder told her the tears had not stopped, but she was barely audible anymore. Matthew's relief was palpable as he settled back down, his back against the bush's spine. Gisella wondered if he had even attempted to sleep yet. Her eyes were gritty by the time Rebecca fell asleep, her relaxed body pulling uncomfortably against Gisella's arms.

Careful not to disturb Rebecca, she laid her back on the ground, holding her breath until she was certain her heavy breathing hadn't altered. Resting back on her heels, she glanced toward Matthew, and his sad gaze met her own.

"Thank you." His voice was barely a murmur, but it eased the strain between her shoulders. "I didn't know what to do." He scoffed, shaking his head. "I think I can get us through these woods, and we'll soon learn whether or not I'm right. But I took one look at her, and I was lost. Crying girls have always confounded me." His voice was light almost as if it were meant to be a joke, but his eyes were too grief-stricken. He had younger sisters, a few years younger than Gisella, but older than Rebecca.

She could nearly see his guilt weighing on his shoulders. He had left his sisters behind when he had slipped away from home that morning. He probably excused them for being too young to bring along, when in reality, Gisella knew it was because he hadn't wanted them there. Much like she hadn't told Malachi because he would have told Papa. They didn't want their siblings there to ruin their fun this morning. And now they would never be there.

"All she wanted was comfort." She wiped her nose with her apron. "I can understand the need." She attempted a shaky smile but Matthew didn't return the effort.

"Thank you, nonetheless."

She nodded and returned to her spot by Silas. The autumn grass was prickly against her arms as she lay down. Her ears listened for any discomfort from Rebecca, but to her relief, the young girl had surrendered to her exhaustion. At least for a few hours, she might rest in oblivion.

Her eyes had barely shut before another sob rang out in the night. She rose again as Winnie cried in Matthew's arms. He attempted to rock her back and forth, but his movements were stilted and uncomfortable.

When Gisella approached, he handed Winnie over without a word. She repeated the same pattern she had with Rebecca and soon Winnie was able to sleep heavily again. Twice more, the pattern occurred, with both Georges, each sob drawing her from sleep.

Matthew was always there before she was, easing worries before giving them to Gisella for the comfort they so desperately sought. It wasn't simple or easy, and every turn in her pacing was met with more tears until her eyes felt as if sand had been rubbed into them. She walked less and less, beginning to rock back and forth on her feet not trusting her ability to keep from stumbling.

With bleary eyes, she settled down once more, finally not to be woken by another's cry as she muffled her own and let her exhaustion overcome her.

The next day dawned far too brightly, in Gisella's opinion. Her mind was a cloud of grief and sadness and yet the sun broke the horizon with a determination she envied. Silas had pressed in close to her in the early morning hours, and she tried her best not to wake him as she rose and moved toward the beautyberries.

Without a word, Matthew followed behind her and they settled into their freshly-developed routine. As they divided their collected loot and distributed it among the dirty hands and hungry stomachs, she noticed more than a few faces had tear tracks striping their cheeks. She could tell the younger children weren't the only ones who had spent their night forlornly.

Her heart ached with the evidence of grief she saw. Her feet dragged as she helped Silas to his feet. He had become her responsibility since she had carried him yesterday. It seemed the same throughout their makeshift camp; the pairs Matthew had made now remained together.

The day began the same as the last had ended. The silence of their routine fell over them once more. If it weren't for the memory of Rebecca's sobs and George's late-night whimpers, she would have questioned whether they had ever stopped at all.

The late September heat drained her energy quickly; the berries that had made up supper and breakfast were quick to dissipate in her stomach. When it was next their turn, she had to tug on Silas' hand twice as he stared longingly toward a clump of berries glistening faraway in a clearing. Clearly, her stomach wasn't the only one protesting.

When Matthew ducked into the shelter, she halted him with a hand on his arm. "We're going to need more than the berries we had this morning if we want to keep up this pace."

His eyes narrowed as he surveyed the group and slowly shook his head. "I wish we could—believe me. But not only do we not have time to spare to search for something else, but we don't even have a knife between all of us." His gaze turned apologetic. "We're stuck with berries."

"I understand," she nodded but continued stalling his next step. "But if you're considering our next shelter and there is an option next to a berry bush," she paused, uncertain how to finish her statement without sounding ungrateful for his efforts up until now. "I think most of us can manage to eat and walk at the same time."

"I'll see what I can do." A hint of a smile twitched Matthew's lips before he turned and disappeared once more.

It was another four shelters along before a blackberry bush brushed up against the grove of sycamores. The first in their group began picking them upon their arrival and were still ready to leave once John and Rebecca arrived.

Gisella grabbed several handfuls, using her apron as a giant pocket. To her surprise, Silas looked up from the hoard of berries he had been eating and began dropping those he picked into her apron as well.

When it was their turn, Gisella tucked Charlotte's hand into her apron and grabbed a handful of berries with her free hand. Ducking from the leaves, she slipped her handful of berries into John's unsuspecting hand. A whispered thank you followed as she grabbed another handful as they walked. Before ducking between the sycamore trunks she slipped up behind Matthew, her hand brushed his fingers as she transferred the berries.

For a moment, his startled gaze met hers. She didn't know if she should be offended at his surprise. As if he had expected her to forget about the lack of time he had to fill his own stomach. With a simple nod, she stepped between the sycamore trees, satisfied to have done something to help

The sun was at its peak when the smell of smoke tickled Gisella's nose. Her head swung in the direction of the wind, but the woods remained as still as they had been all morning. No flames licked toward them, but the scent was unmistakable on the air. It swept from the direction they fled, adding a hint of foreboding to an already gravely silent group.

She caught Matthew's concerned gaze as he glanced behind her, but he didn't speak. No one did. The silence rang on as the smell of smoke thickened. It wasn't long until they began to see smoke.

It hung low in the air, its wispy fingers clutching the ground tightly. The forest behind them became hazier, and the wind kicked up fiercer, pushing it toward them with haste.

"We have to move faster." Matthew's tone brooked no argument as they hunched below the low branches of the dogwood bushes.

"How? Even if we carry the younger ones, the fire might catch up to us." John turned into the wind, his brow furrowed as if he could see the flames beyond the hazy horizon.

"I know, and this wind isn't going to help." Matthew heaved a breath before rubbing a hand across his eyes. The smoky air was starting to sting Gisella's eyes as well, but she guessed Matthew's exhaustion had something to do with it also. The boy had stayed up at least as long as she had last night, most likely longer, in order to keep watch.

"We're going to have to abandon hiding." The words seemed to be pulled reluctantly from Matthew's mouth. Gisella rocked back in surprise, she caught Elias and James exchanging surprised glances as well.

"It's the only way," said John, sighing resignedly.

"All right, but we'll maintain the same order we've been moving in this whole time. First, always keep a hiding spot in sight. Even though we won't be able to slink from one spot to the next, I expect everyone to have a destination in mind should they need it at a moment's notice." All of the kids, excluding Charlotte nodded; even young Winnie imitated James' motion.

"Secondly, we'll be carrying the younger ones. For now, speed is our ally; the faster we move, the better chance we have of getting away from that fire. Now, let's split up and get moving." It only took a few breaths for everyone to shuffle into order.

A minute later, they stepped out of the bushes. Matthew led the way, the younger George clinging to his back while he held Rebecca in his arms. This left John to carry the older George and Elias to walk under his own power with Martin beside him. Everyone else stayed with who they had helped the day before.

Stepping out into the open without a destination to scurry to felt odd and far too exposed. A shiver crawled down Gisella's spine as Charlotte tucked her hand into her apron strings once more and Silas clasped his arms tightly around her neck.

She tried to focus on good hiding places should the need arise, but her gaze kept skipping frantically between the trees. It was as if each tree trunk had eyes and they were all looking at her. After a day and a half of hiding, she disliked the open space as she followed Matthew's unfaltering lead.

The faster and farther they moved, the more her heart ached

until its throbbing was as consistent as her footsteps. As the day lengthened, the smoke maintained its intensity, it didn't lessen despite their quicker pace. When the sun fell behind the trees, Matthew sped up his steps once more, desperately fleeing the one truth they all understood. If there was fire, it would spread.

Their disheartened band accepted the new pace without question. Gisella worried about the reticence of the younger children. Where yesterday had been full of sobs, today was silent.

Her eyes grew bleary as the sunlight dampened and long shadows crept across the ground. Her focus remained on Matthew, forcing herself to hold onto Silas a little longer—to ignore the pain in her arms and the stiffness in her fingers. Gisella couldn't understand how Matthew's feet strode so confidently; her own dragged slower with every step. But she made them continue on, no longer pausing when her petticoat caught on an underlying thorn. A torn petticoat was the least of her concerns.

The smoke never fully disbanded, but finally, Matthew motioned to halt once the last vestiges of daylight were bleeding from the sky. Silence reigned as they prepared to bed on the grass once more; a nearby creek allowed for fresh water, something that had been scarce in the last two days. Gisella guessed Matthew had also chosen the position for safety, if the fire were to creep upon them during the night, they could always retreat to the water.

Silas had woken up not long before they stopped for the night, and he scrambled down quickly. She envied his energy. After having been carried most of the day and being able to sleep for a few hours, his body was far more rested than her own.

Charlotte settled with her back to a dense bush a few paces

away. Gisella inhaled deeply, her nose twitching at the smoky scent. For a moment, she relished the solitude with both Charlotte and Silas occupied. She rolled her head side to side, nearly wincing at the tight pull of her shoulders. Silas might be young, but his gangly height definitely didn't make carrying him easy.

Her gaze wandered around their makeshift camp in the haze of dusk, taking in its exhausted occupants. Her battered heart squeezed at the empty faces sitting around her. There had once been life and light in each of their eyes. Laughter had fallen from their lips easier than words. She wondered if it would ever return.

Desperate for a distraction, Gisella ensured Silas was occupied with the younger of the Georges before searching out Matthew. He stood next to John, speaking in low tones. "Shouldn't we have reached the next settlement by now?" she interrupted, her voice pitched low so only they could hear.

John nodded, his eyes heavy as he glanced back at Matthew. "The wind shifted after midday. The smoke was also coming from the east."

Her breath stuttered in her lungs. East, toward New Bern, toward every settlement they were headed toward.

"I don't want to lead us into what we barely escaped."

She and John nodded in agreement. Dusk reigned in the woods, but she was glad she could make out more beautyberry bushes nearby. They would survive on berries alone if need be.

John voiced the question that burned on her tongue. "What do we do if they're all gone?"

"We won't find out." Matthew's voice took on a hard edge. "I shifted our path as soon as I noticed the shift in the wind. If we stay on this course, we should pass south of every settlement and avoid any destruction there."

"But where are we going?" Gisella tried to calm the fear creeping into her voice. "We can't live in the woods forever. We need homes." Her voice broke. Her mind conjured up an image of home, a place of warmth and love. She would never go home again, and her heart broke at the realization.

Without a word, Matthew wrapped an arm around her shoulders. She wished she could be as strong as he was. In the two days of leading, his back had stood straight and tall, never wavering as he pulled each kid from their wallowing and led them toward hope—toward life.

"There will be search parties sent out, once news gets back east." His boots scuffed the leaves underfoot. "We walk and we pray we run into one of them."

John nodded resolutely, averting his red-rimmed eyes. "It's the best way to control who finds us and not be caught off guard." Gisella sniffled loudly as they remained in their cluster. There was nothing left to say, but the break from the thoughts in her own head made her reluctant to break away.

Her gaze flitted to Charlotte. Her friend sat where she had left her, eyes swollen from tears and paler than last night's moon . She hadn't spoken a word since they had left yesterday.

With a smile of thanks, she shifted from Matthew's side and made her way to her silent friend. Charlotte's golden hair was limp against her back, the braid it had been pulled back in no longer visible.

"Do you want to talk?" Gisella whispered as gently as she

could. She didn't know what else to say.

Charlotte shook her head emphatically. Gisella waited to see if she would do anything else, but she had returned to staring at the ground beneath her boots. Without another word, Gisella went to collect another meal of berries. There were plenty to choose from, and she said a prayer of gratitude they were ripe and in season.

When her apron was bulging with berries, she took them around the group, handing as many as she could to each child, doing her best to ignore the red eyes and blank stares. When all that remained was her and Silas' portion she sat back on the ground beside him.

Silas' dark hair highlighted his slender face, despite being barely seven years old. His family had been new to the settlement. Gisella tried not to think about his younger sisters or their glaring absence.

Water flooded her eyes as she looked around the group. Everyone sat near each other, but there was no camaraderie. They might look like a group, but they were all separate, all alone. Even Matthew's head hung low, his arms slung across his knees.

Unable to bear the sight any longer, she scooted across the few feet separating her from Charlotte and took her hand in her own. Silas shifted with her, maintaining their close proximity . Desperate for hope—for some warmth of spirit—Gisella threw her arm around his shoulders. His bony body was anything but soft, yet her heart melted as he relaxed against her.

It was all she could do, but maybe Charlotte and Silas would find comfort in knowing they weren't entirely alone. Gisella most certainly did.

The night passed in much the same manner as the previous

one, with sobs interrupting her sleep. She wasn't sure if it was the exhaustion or some small portion of acceptance, but each crying child's sorrow eased a little quicker that night, their weight becoming heavier in her arms. To her relief, Matthew slept that night and John took up his unwavering post instead.

She understood the need to be on watch to be able to see any surprises before they were upon them, especially with the threatening smoke sitting heavy in the air. But her heart ached for both boys who had shouldered the responsibilities of men. When the younger George had settled back down, she returned to her place by Silas, dropping a gentle hand on John's head as she passed. His grateful smile eased some of her worry as she sank into the dirt and swiftly fell asleep.

The next morning as she handed out berries, she made an effort to try and touch each person—a pat on the shoulder, a squeeze of the hand, a ruffle of another's hair. It wasn't much, but the contact helped ease some of the pain inside her.

She was on the older side of their group but there were a few the same age as her, James, and Martin. Charlotte, John, and Matthew, each two or three years above them.

That day, she remained observant as they continued in a single file line. Having not run into any issues fleeing the fire yesterday, it had been determined that speed was more necessary than stealth, at least for the moment. Gisella was grateful to see a few less vacant stares among the group. Her heart warmed as Martin helped George over a stream and little Rebecca onto John's back without being prompted. It was almost as if the entire group was awakening from a deep sleep.

Gisella wished what they were running from was as easily swept aside as a nightmare.

Gray clouds hung low all morning, pressing the smoky air tighter to the ground. There were moments when the haze made her eyes water only for a breeze to whisk the worst of it away a heartbeat later. Only once half the day had passed did the rain begin its inevitable fall. The first drop hit her squarely on the shoulder. She shivered as another dropped along the back of her neck.

She turned her face up to the sky only to get a splash of water on her face. The droplets began to fall in earnest, and she tilted her head down, wishing she hadn't abandoned her bonnet back in the meadow.

Matthew and the other boys had to brush their wet hair from their eyes as they kept moving forward. Their pace slowed significantly as they plodded along, Gisella's hemline growing dark with mud.

When they were all thoroughly soaked through, Matthew halted the group, motioning toward a cluster of sycamore trees. The broad leaves blocked some of the water but not much as they huddled near the trunks. The sound of rain increased, and Silas shivered against Gisella.

Glancing around, she settled down at the base of the tree. It would be some time before they were moving again, and her feet would appreciate the break. The wet leaves of the forest floor soaked into her thin petticoats, but her feet throbbed in relief.

Without warning, Silas climbed onto her lap facing her with a stubborn set to his chin.

"Hello, Silas," she whispered, uncertain what he needed.

Without a word, he tucked his head under her chin, settling heavily against her. Surprised, she gently reached her arms around him. His wet hair tickled her neck as she watched the water fall through the woods.

The murmur of feet on wet leaves pulled her from her absentminded state as Rebecca and the older George approached. Without a word, they settled in at her side. Rebecca leaned her head against Gisella's shoulder, and George closed his eyes, tilting his head against the tree trunk beside her. A whisper of a laugh reached her ears and she turned to see Matthew watching their tiny gathering.

Before she could respond, Winnie settled on her free side. She wrapped both arms around Gisella's arm and snuggled in tightly. Her breath caught in her throat as the little girl relaxed, her body turning to the consistency of a mud puddle.

Tears stung her eyes, but for the first time in three days it was not sadness weighing her down, but happiness and relief. She murmured a grateful prayer that her presence was reassuring to the younger children. It was a wonderful gift to be able to assist. Their circumstances weren't something she could have prevented. Even if she had remained at home like she was supposed to, the only difference would have been her own death. There had been no way to alter the outcome of their circumstances since it began three days ago, she took that moment to enjoy the rare feeling of being useful.

Letting her spine relax, she sank deeper into the tree's bark, ignoring its scratch against her neck. Just as her eyes drifted shut, a gentle wind brushed Silas' hair against her nose. Her body stiffened as she fought an oncoming sneeze.

"What is it?" Matthew's urgent whisper distracted her.

"What?" she replied.

"Did you see or hear something?" His eyes scanned the wet forest rapidly, crouching just on the other side of Winnie.

"I didn't see anything," Gisella replied, confused.

"Then why did you straighten up, your eyes wide?" he asked, his brow furrowed.

"Oh," she felt blood rush into her cheeks. "I had to sneeze and was worried about waking Silas." She murmured, embarrassed at her overreaction.

Matthew's laugh washed over her like a fresh spring during the driest of summers. It had been days since she had heard anything joyful or even the slightest-bit merry. She let herself relax into a giggle, only to have Silas' hair brush her nose once more.

This time there was no fighting the sneeze that tore through her. She barely kept her head from colliding with Silas's. Matthew's laugh lengthened, and she joined in gently, doing her best not to disturb anyone leaning against her. When silence fell once more, her gaze caught Matthew's, and neither of them spoke for a minute.

"Thank you," he whispered.

"For what? Nearly waking everyone up after they finally settled down?" she replied with a tease in her voice, relishing the lighthearted air to their conversation.

But Matthew didn't return her grin; his eyes were serious but thankfully not sad. "For giving them the comfort they so obviously need." With that, he rose from his crouch and wandered away toward John.

Gisella let the smile remain on her lips, enjoying the feeling of warmth and companionship as four smaller bodies pressed in on her. She let her body relax and her mind ease, knowing they just might make it through this.

━━━━━━━━━━━━━━━━━

By the fourth day, gentle conversations interspersed their footsteps as they trekked behind Matthew. They were barely audible whispers, as Matthew had instructed, but they warmed Gisella just the same. After so much silence, any noise was welcome to her ears as her still damp petticoats clung to her legs.

The sun had barely reached its crest when Matthew halted. In an instant, every voice was cut off as everyone held their breath. Gisella waited for the signal to continue. They had done this several times each day but not since the first day had anything come of it.

A twig snapped to the north and Gisella flinched. Meeting her gaze, Matthew pointed to a clump of trees to the south. Knowing what needed to be done, Gisella stepped to the side, a brush of her fingertips drawing each child from their immobile state. Balancing haste and stealth, she slipped nearer to the alcove, relieved to see there were several places to slide through. Motioning the youngest inside, she stood watch as their group dwindled in numbers, disappearing amidst the brush. Her heart raced as she watched Charlotte slip into the opening.

Matthew and John nodded to each other before ducking behind nearby bushes. They distanced themselves slightly from the group, its protectors when there was no protection to be had. Her eyes watered at the action, knowing they would be the first to enter into danger should the Tuscarora arrive.

As Gisella hunkered down into the remaining gap in the clump of trees, she set her feet in determination. She would stand with Matthew and John should the need arise. Her palms sweated against her petticoats, and she prayed the need would not arise.

A whimper sounded behind her but was quickly muffled as the rustling increased. Multiple footsteps could be heard moving closer.

Her sightline was partially obscured by the bush Matthew hid behind. She saw three figures move into the area, but the leaves kept her from seeing anything more distinctive. Instead, she focused on Matthew.

His shoulders tensed, and Gisella shifted her weight to the balls of her feet, ready to move at the slightest indication. Four heartbeats later, Matthew's shoulders relaxed and she nearly collapsed in relief as he raised his head above the bush.

Matthew spoke abruptly, shattering the forest's silence. "Hail there."

"Who goes there?" A man demanded.

"Are you searching for survivors?" Matthew asked, ignoring the man's question. He motioned for Gisella and John to stay down as he stepped from behind the bush.

"That we are," a different voice responded. "You're the first we've come across. Ignore Ol' Hank here; he's been jumpy since the attack."

"Can you blame me, Tim? Them Tuscarora can move like spirits through these trees," Ol' Hank grumbled, but his voice seemed to have softened slightly.

"You all alone?" Tim asked.

She watched Matthew carefully; he had yet to give away their presence. She held her breath as she waited, trusting Matthew to do what was best.

Just then, another set of footsteps interrupted the conversation. These were softer, and she saw the color drain from Matthew's face. Without even being able to see, she knew who had arrived. Matthew took a half step toward their hiding place, before freezing.

"How do I know if I can trust you?" Matthew asked.

A whimper sounded behind Gisella. Recognizing it as Charlotte, it was the only sound she had made since they had left the meadow four days ago. Gisella reached a hand back blindly. She gripped Charlotte's hand and squeezed, trying to give her reassurance without taking her eyes from Matthew.

"What is there to question? We've been searching these woods for two days," Ol' Hank sputtered.

"And him?" Matthew nodded his head toward the newest arrival.

"He had no part in the attack. It was the other mioty of Tuscarora who attacked. Besides, he's been a loyal companion as we have searched. If he had wanted to harm you or us, he would have done so by now," Tim answered with all confidence.

When Matthew didn't respond, Gisella could feel the man's growing impatience. Why she had no idea. He wasn't the one who had been foraging for berries and surviving in the woods for the last four days.

"Who's hiding?"

Gisella quailed at the familiar accent. It was the same pronunciation she had heard that fateful day before dawn. She saw John visibly shudder. The few Tuscarora in their settlement who had adopted her language had always had a distinct way of turning it over in their mouth.

"We will need to search the surrounding area to look for more survivors, whether or not you trust us. That is the job we were *all* tasked with." Tim emphasized confidently.

There was a pregnant pause.

"Gisella." Matthew turned his head toward her and nodded.

She rose swiftly stepping out to find four men watching her curiously. Turning around she helped Charlotte out with a shaky smile. She did the same for every member of their tired band, trying to encourage them. Perhaps the nightmare was over; perhaps this was the end of their ordeal. She knew they would never be the same for it, but perhaps a touch of normalcy would now interweave with it.

Silas was the last to leave the alcove, and she clasped hands with him as they walked to where Matthew stood facing the men. John took his place on the other side of Matthew as if to block the men from fully seeing the group congregating behind him.

The wide eyes of all the men would have been comical in other circumstances. To Gisella, it showed how hopeless they had been to find any survivors. It left little to wonder what they had found at the sites of the attacks.

"So many," Tim whispered with an awestruck look in his gaze. "Thank the merciful Lord for it."

Ol' Hank added his own amen.

"Where are we?" Matthew asked, his eyes still scanning the group calculatingly.

"You're about three miles south of New Bern," Ol' Hank replied as he shuffled his feet in the leaves. "Where did you start from?"

"Forty miles upriver," said John, speaking for the first time, his voice resolute. Gisella could see his jaw was locked, holding back the emotions that had been eating at all of them. Grief passed over his gaze for a moment.

There had been no established name for their settlement, but she saw the recognition in the men's faces all the same. A heartbeat of silence passed, thick with unspoken words.

"Let's get you back to town," Tim muttered.

"Is it still there?" Matthew asked, halting the group mid-turn. They exchanged glances before the Tuscaroran replied.

"Enough of it is."

Without another word, they began their trek toward New Bern.

━━━━━━━━━━━━━━

Whether it was the promise of a destination or the revival of new companions, their sorry band moved with a lighter step as they entered New Bern. The settlement looked especially dirty in the day's waning light as if it had been coated in smoke.

Matthew's step slowed beside her own, and she could practically feel the relief slough off him in waves. This had been their goal. For four days, they had fought to stay together, to stay alive so they could reach this point. All their work to find this community and safety.

Without thought, Gisella linked her arm through Matthew's. They had never expected to live through what they experienced. But they had survived. Together.

Tears filled her eyes as they stepped into the settlement. While bigger than home, it had much the same look. Everything was newly constructed yet hardly clean or fresh-looking. The packed dirt of the road they walked on warmed the soles of Gisella's boots and she nearly began crying at the thought of being able to take them off. After so long in them, she wouldn't be surprised if her feet were stuck in them for good.

Surprised stares met them as Ol' Hank, a portly man of indiscernible years, led them toward the easily identifiable church meeting house. She could hear the whispers rippling through those who looked on.

The creak of the door opening pulled a wide grin from Gisella. They were finally going to be inside. She had always hated sleeping outdoors. The trip from the coast up the river had been unsavory and endless. When Papa had finally finished constructing their house, she had never been happier. That same sweep of joy and relief swaddled her as she and Matthew followed at the back of the group.

The room was empty save for pews and Ol' Hank, who had removed his hat. Standing near the front, he shuffled his feet, suddenly nervous under their watchful eyes.

"Go ahead and settle in here, for the time being." He picked at his hat idly. "I'll go and see what's to be done with you." With a hesitant nod, he ambled from the building.

Silence followed after him filled with questions. The young

survivors glanced back and forth between each other uncertainly. Since fleeing four days ago, they had had one goal driving them, survival until a search party found them. But now their goal had been accomplished there was a listlessness in their party that hadn't been present before.

"Idle hands make for an idle mind." The gentle whisper wove through Gisella's mind as clear as if Mama were standing right next to her. Focusing on the wisdom of the words and not the sharp pang in her heart, Gisella nodded resolutely.

"I would suspect we'll be spending the night here. I need everyone to choose a pew they would like to claim as a bed tonight." Her voice wavered, and she cleared her throat as if it were just a weak tickle bothering her. She spoke over the sudden rustle of movement as boots scuffed the packed dirt floor. "You may go ahead and remove your stockings and boots."

As each occupant found their pew, Gisella made her way to one of the few remaining at the rear of the church. Matthew and John had taken the final two pews in the church immediately next to the doors. She smiled gently at them as she sat down on her empty pew.

A sigh slipped from her lips as her feet swung from the bench. The solid wood under her was far from soft, but she had never been more grateful for a piece of furniture. Moving slowly, she toed off her boots, relishing the brush of fresh air as she stripped her stockings off next. She flexed and wiggled her toes.

For a moment, there was silence. It wasn't the heavy and oppressive lack of voices that had haunted them for so many days. Instead, it was the silence of relief—of exhaustion—after a trial had been overcome.

Murmurs of conversations broke out soon, and Gisella let herself enjoy her solitude for a few moments more before she turned back toward Matthew.

"What do we do now?" she asked.

He shrugged, his eyes not quite meeting hers. His long legs were stretched out on the floor before him. The tips of his toes were red from rubbing against his boots.

"I think we should pray." John's suggestion surprised her. He had always been the one trying to get out of church functions, dodging his mother's iron grip as he darted outside. "I think it might be good to give thanks…" He paused, his throat bobbing. "And to remember," he finished softly.

Gisella couldn't argue his point nor did she want to. Maybe prayer was what they needed. Maybe it was what Charlotte needed.

Matthew nodded and stood. His groan as his weight shifted to his feet made Gisella smile. She knew her feet would protest just as strongly.

Within a few minutes, they had everyone gathered at the front of the room in a loose circle. Reaching out to Charlotte and Silas on either side of her, Gisella gripped their hands and bowed her head.

John led the simple prayer. The words weren't elaborate but simple and true. The catch in his voice was met with sniffles and tears. Gently, John led the recitation of each family member's name. It took three tries for George to say his brother's name, and Matthew's voice was so hoarse she could barely understand his words. Charlotte remained silent when it was her turn, her hand shaking in Gisella's. It was only after she offered to say the names in Charlotte's stead that the shaking subsided to a tremor.

When John said the final amen, her heart throbbed painfully, as if she had spent the time prodding at it with a sharp stick. But as she looked around at those sitting next to her, the pain that had been embedded in her heart like a burr on her skin was gone. She took a full breath, savoring the warmth that suffused her blood. It felt an awful lot like hope.

Ol' Hank cleared his throat, and the bustle of the meeting house died down. It had been four days since they arrived in New Bern. The church meeting house had become a home to Gisella and her fellows, but that was about to change.

The fluttering in her stomach wouldn't abate as she sat on one of the two front pews with all her friends. Ol' Hank had informed them last night they would be divided among households today. Silas clung to her waist tightly, and she tried to rub soothing circles across his shoulders, but the motion didn't seem to be easing his worry.

"We would like to express once more our gratitude to the Lord for keeping you children safe in this trialsome hour." Ol' Hank looked fondly down on where they sat. Since they had arrived, he had been their most common visitor and source of information. "The time has come to divide you amongst your foster families. These lovely people have opened their homes to you, and I expect you to return that action with gratitude. As a community, we expect you to work with your family and assist them in their sustenance and craft."

"Yes, sir," Gisella murmured along with the others.

"Excellent." Wrinkles formed around his eyes as he smiled affectionately. And with that, he began to call out names, attaching them to families. Both Georges were sent to live with a magistrate. Gisella was glad to see Rebecca and Winnie were chosen to live with a young farmer and his wife who lived on the outskirts of town. She knew the two girls would be as thick of thieves for many years.

John and Martin were to live with the pastor and his elderly sister. Elias went to a trader, and Silas went to the town's tanner. His hands gripped Gisella tighter, and she wished for his sake that he wasn't going somewhere alone.

Pulling him onto her lap, she let him cling to her for what would likely be the last time. Her heart ached at his obvious despair. He had lost so much already; she hated that she wouldn't be with him to help him further.

But each of these families was helping the only way they could; there would be a limited amount of food in each home. She couldn't expect each family to take in multiple mouths to feed. Despite the logic, a few tears trickled down her nose as she waited for her own assignment.

"Gisella and Charlotte." Ol' Hank glanced at each girl in turn. "You will be staying with the Johansons, our town blacksmith." Charlotte made no reaction to the announcement. Her ever-present blank gaze focused across the room. When Ol' Hank looked at her, Gisella nodded her understanding, espying the large man near the back of the room.

"And lastly, Matthew and James will be going with the Larsons." The two boys nodded as they glanced at the land surveyor seriously.

Silas's muffled cries were the only sound in the room before Ol' Hank cleared his throat once more. "I know this parting is not easy. Not after you have already had to give up so much. But I would ask you to look toward the break in the clouds. You will be able to live here in New Bern together. And while you may not see each other every day, weekly services will grant you the chance to regroup. And I think that is a blessing, don't you?" Ol' Hank didn't wait for an answer and turned to the magistrate, taking both Georges and beginning a conversation with him.

Voices filled the room, and all too soon, Silas's new family approached. The woman looked to be a few years older than Mama had been, the man several years older. Their faces looked worn—like a well-used apron—but the woman's smile was ready and genuine.

"Come now, Silas," she intoned as she gently took hold of his shoulder.

Sliding from Gisella's lap, he straightened his shoulders. His nose was snotty and Gisella wiped the last vestiges of it away with her apron.

"I will see you soon, Silas." Her voice broke on his name, and she leaned forward to kiss his forehead. For a moment, she lingered with her head pressed against his.

It was harder to let go than she had expected. She had wanted to return to a semblance of normalcy, but it was hard to watch Silas walk out the door. Winnie and Rebecca weren't far behind, clutching each other's hands like a lifeline.

"I guess this is it." The gentle words brought her eyes from the door. Matthew didn't move his gaze as the pair of Georges trailed behind their new family and out into the open air.

"I guess so," she whispered. She took a moment to study him. Guilt still hung about him like a cloud. She wished there was something she could say to disband it, but deep down, she knew her words would do no good. Some weights must be dealt with alone, and Matthew's couldn't be swept away by words.

"Thank you." His sharp green eyes found hers.

"You were the one to lead us; I would have gotten us lost in the woods." She tried for a smile and was glad when it only shook slightly.

"True," he agreed with a grin. "You're not good with directions." He tugged lightly on one of her braids, and her heart lifted at his teasing.

Before they had to flee, this was the only side of Matthew she had known. Now, she had seen a far different side, one that could take on the responsibilities of an adult. She respected the serious side for its abilities, but she was giddy to see his teasing side. It meant that some small part of him had survived that day.

"But I don't think we would have made it without your assistance." He shook his head slowly, scuffing a toe on the ground.

"Thank you," she whispered. "We make a good team." Matthew's returning smile was bright and full, embedding a sliver of happiness into her sore heart.

"That we do." With a nod, he was off, following James and Mr. Larson toward their new home.

Turning, she gathered her thoughts. Charlotte sat where she had left her. Her friend had shown no interest in the world around her since their arrival. Again and again, Gisella had tried to speak with her but to no avail.

She saw Mr. Johanson approach from his place by Ol' Hank. Moving to Charlotte, she pulled her to a standing position, determined to face her future resolutely. But she was glad to have her best friend by her side.

"Who is who?" Mr. Johanson asked gruffly.

"I am Gisella, and this is Charlotte." Gisella swallowed down her nerves and hid the slight shake in her hands as she grabbed Charlotte's. "Thank you for taking us into your home." Just because Mama wasn't here didn't mean she could ignore the manners she had been taught.

Mr. Johanson merely nodded and headed out the door. Straightening her shoulders, Gisella stepped after him toward her future. Whatever that may hold.

HISTORICAL NOTE:

At dawn on September 22, 1711, one mioty (one of two groupings within the tribe) of the Tuscarora in what is now eastern North Carolina attacked the settlers living there. Despite not having the full support of their tribe, the Tuscarora led the attack with collaboration from multiple other tribes.

Just as Gisella and her friends were taken by surprise, the settlers had no warning of the attack. Many of the Tuscarora entered the settlements the night before, under the pretense of asking for food and drink, to be in position at dawn. No settlers were spared for age or sex, and those who hid were flushed out by fire. Some of the attackers came from within, as Indians who worked and lived within some of the settlers' homes rose up against them. Records are not clear regarding how many died that day, as settlements were abandoned with the dead left unburied, but most accounts estimate that 130 were killed.

The Tuscarora gained possession of the "firewater" rum as the massacre commenced, which led to three days of bloodshed. The town of New Bern was the last settlement to be attacked around nightfall on September 22, and it is estimated one-third of the population of New Bern was killed.

The band of children who survived this attack is not

fictionalized. George Conis and George Kneegee, both of whose names are alluded to in this story, were found with a group of children by a search party sent out from New Bern after the attack. How they came to survive an attack where no others were spared remains unknown. This could have been the result of mercy on the part of some of the attackers, or they could have escaped by their own means as played out in this story. Upon arrival at New Bern, both Georges were fostered by Captain Jacob Miller, an early magistrate and presiding justice in Craven County.

While the attack itself was unexpected, there had been rising tensions in the area over land encroachment by the settlers as well as the raiding of villages, which resulted in many Tuscarora being enslaved. The September 22 attack sparked the "Tuscarora War," which would last until 1713. It would claim the lives of many colonists as well as a large number of Tuscaroran men. The captured Tuscaroran women and children were primarily sold into slavery.

By the end of the war, the Tuscarora left the area. They joined with the Five Nations in Pennsylvania, becoming the sixth and final member.

REFERENCES:

Primary Sources: These are sources that existed at or near the time of the event. These are always the best sources to rely on, as they are based on first-hand experience and/or initial perceptions. The greater the length of time between a source's creation date and the event, the less value it has. Perceptions of history change and flow depending on current circumstances and often create filters through which history is viewed. For this reason, primary sources should always hold sway over secondary sources.

Secondary Sources: These are sources that offer commentary on a past event or situation. These are often well-researched and base their findings on primary sources. However, they are created in order to push an argument or an idea; they are rarely created to simply tell a story. This makes them less trustworthy, and they should be used cautiously.

Primary Sources:

Letters of Chief Justice Christopher Gale, written November 1711.

Secondary Sources:

The North Carolina Booklet – Great Events in North Carolina History: Indian Massacre and Tuscarora War – Judge Walter Clark. Published July 1902.

Indians Massacre Neuse and Trent River Settlers – Bonnie Edwards. Published March 1998 in The Olde Kinston Gazette.

The Tuscarora War: Indians, Settlers, and the Fight for the Carolina Colonies – David La Vere. Published August 1, 2016.

Check out L.C. Rusch's website at www.lcrusch.com for the latest updates to the *I'm American* series and extras on the research and writing process for each story!

Don't forget to review this story and help other readers find it!

www.ingramcontent.com/pod-product-compliance
Lightning Source LLC
LaVergne TN
LVHW051818080426
835513LV00017B/1997